The *Prince* and the *Pauper*

Mark Twain

Adapted by Susanna Davidson

Illustrated by Katie Pamment

Reading Consultant: Alison Kelly
Roehampton University

Contents

I will set down a tale as it was told to me by one who had it from his father, who had it from HIS father, who had it from HIS father — and so on, back and still back, three hundred years and more. It may be history, it may be only a legend. It may have happened, it may not have happened: but it COULD have happened.

Mark Twain

Chapter 1

Tom's troubles begin

Tom Canty dragged his feet
as he turned the corner into
Offal Court.

Foul smells oozed from the houses
and ragged children ran screaming
everywhere. Tom climbed the stairs
to a room on the third floor and
pushed open the door.

"Did you get any money?" asked
his father, as soon as he saw him.
Tom held out his empty hands
and shook his head.

"A whole day's begging and nothing to show for it," snarled his father. He swiped at Tom, pushing him into a corner.

"Here," whispered his mother, sneaking over and passing Tom a stale crust of bread.

5

Under a threadbare blanket, Tom nibbled on the bread, then tried to sleep. But his pounding head and tired feet kept him awake.

At last, though, Tom's thoughts began to drift to his dream world. Here, his home was a palace and he was a prince, surrounded by music and riches.

Waking in the cold light of day,
the stench of his family's room
seemed worse than ever.

As he walked the streets of
London that morning, Tom tried
his hardest to block out his life,
and live instead in his dreams.

Without thinking, he wandered
away from the twisting, stinking
streets of his home to Westminster...
and the king's palace.

"Maybe I'll see the prince,"
thought Tom. He joined the people
watching splendid carriages
driving in and out of the palace.

Tom drew closer to the gold-studded bars of the entrance gates and gasped with pleasure. There, in the palace gardens, was the prince.

He was dressed in silks and satins and shining jewels. "If only I could touch him," thought Tom, stretching out his hand.

"Hey!" yelled a soldier, snatching at Tom and throwing him onto the ground.

The onlookers laughed at him. "Look at you, beggar boy!" someone cried. "Keep your filthy hands off the prince."

But the prince was furious. "How dare you!" he shouted at the soldier. "Bring that boy here at once."

Tom was picked up like a feather and carried back to the palace gates.

"I am Edward, Prince of Wales," said the boy. "You've been treated badly, I'm sorry. Would you like to see the palace?"

Tom could only nod.

Chapter 2

Into the palace

"This must be a dream," Tom told himself, as he followed the prince down the palace corridors. He gazed around him in wonder.

What's your name?

Tom Canty, sir.

Finally, they came to a vast room. "Are you hungry?" asked the prince.

"Aren't I always?" said Tom. "I mean, yes, Your Highness..."

Prince Edward ordered a servant to bring food, and water so Tom could wash his hands and face. Tom ignored the water, and gobbled down the food.

"He's so dirty," thought the prince. "He eats like an animal."

"Ooh!" said Tom, still chewing his food. "This room must be at least twenty times bigger than the one we live in."

"You live in a *room*?" asked Prince Edward.

"Yes, all six of us – my parents, sisters and my gran."

The prince looked so shocked, Tom had to laugh. "But life's not all bad. In summer I get to swim in the river and play in the mud."

There's nothing better than wallowing in mud.

"Oh!" said the prince, longingly. "I'd love to strip off my royal robes, just for one moment, and splash in the mud with no one to stop me..."

"And if for one moment I could take off my rags and put on your royal clothes, sir..." said Tom.

"Let's swap clothes, Tom Canty," cried the prince. "But please," he added, "wash first!"

Once Tom had scrubbed himself down, Tom and the prince stood side by side, in front of the mirror, each wearing the other's clothes.

They looked at each other, then they looked into the mirror again. Prince Edward touched Tom's hair, his face... and gasped.

"We're identical," Tom said. "You could be me and I could be you."

"No!" cried the prince. "You're a pauper! I was born to be king!"

"S-s-sorry, Your Highness," stammered Tom. "I didn't mean..."

But the prince's attention was caught by the sight of a livid purple bruise on Tom's arm. "Who did this to you?" he asked.

"Only the soldier," Tom replied. "It's nothing."

But he spoke to thin air. The prince had darted across the room, then disappeared down a corridor.

When the soldier saw the prince, he laughed and pushed him away.

"Who do you think you are?" said the prince, storming up to him. "How dare you touch the Prince of Wales?"

"You deserve to be hanged for this," the prince went on.

"Who do you think *you* are, dressed like that?" jeered the crowd. "Let's get him!"

The prince looked up. He saw people all around him, bearing down on him with their fists raised. He started to run, his bare feet flying as he tried to escape.

When at last he lost them,
Prince Edward looked around
and realized he was lost himself.

His feet were bleeding and
it had begun to rain. He was about
to sink to the ground when he felt a
hand on his shoulder.

"You lazy cur!" boomed a voice in his ear. "Why aren't you begging like you should be? You're coming home for a beating."

"Who are you? Let me go!" cried the prince.

"Who am I?" said the man, laughing. "You can't pretend not to know John Canty – your own *father*!"

Chapter 3

The king is dead

After Prince Edward had left,
Tom stayed in front of the mirror,
admiring his reflection.

24

But as the minutes ticked by, he began to worry. "Where's the prince gone?" he wondered. "What happens if they find me here?"

At last the door opened, to let in a richly dressed girl with flaming red hair, who curtsied to him. Tom trembled before her.

"What's the matter, my lord?" asked the girl.

"I'm not *my lord*," said Tom. "I'm Tom Canty – a pauper."

The girl laughed.

"What tricks are you playing on your sister?" she asked.

"My sister?" gasped Tom. "Are you Princess Elizabeth?"

Tom instantly fell to his knees. Elizabeth came over to him, a worried frown on her face.

"What is it, my lord?" she asked.

"Don't call me that!" cried Tom, whimpering. "I told you – I'm Tom Canty. I'm a pauper, not a prince."

Elizabeth hurried from the room. In no time, a whisper was racing around the palace – "The prince has lost his mind!"

Tom ran and hid behind a chair. "They'll come and get me now," he thought, terror-struck. "They'll hang me for sure."

When the door opened again, a grandly dressed noble entered the room. He bowed to Tom and beckoned to him. "Come, nephew," he said. "Your father would like to see you."

Helplessly, Tom followed him. Servants bowed to him along the way and Tom tried to bow back.

When they reached the king's room, Tom hung back behind the nobles. He was shocked to see the king looked old and sick. He had tiny, puffy eyes in a flushed and swollen face.

"Lord Hertford?" said the king. "Have you brought my son?"

Lord Hertford pushed Tom forward.

"Don't be afraid," said the king, his voice sounding faint and wheezy. "I'm your father who loves you. Come to me."

"P-p-please, Your Majesty," Tom stammered. "Can I go?"

"Go where?" asked the king.

"Back home, to Offal Court."

The king clasped Tom to him. "So it's true," he muttered. "You have lost your mind."

He glared at all the courtiers, who were watching with interest. "It won't last!" he shouted. "He has studied too much, that is all. Stop him from studying and he'll recover. Now go! I am tired."

"But what about the Duke of Norfolk?" asked a lord. "He's still in the Tower. We need your decision..."

The king clutched his chest, as if in great pain, then gasped, "Hang him tomorrow. It's what he deserves."

"Hanged?" thought Tom. "If that's what they do to a duke, what will they do to me? How can I tell them who I really am? I'll be trapped here forever..."

At Offal Court, the prince was thinking the same thing. He stood in a corner of the cold, bare room, watching Tom's sisters sleeping in the dirty straw.

Tom's mother kept trying to comfort him.

"Let me go," he begged her. "I'm not your son. I'm Edward, Prince of Wales."

"Shh!" Tom's mother replied. "Please stop saying that. You'll only make your father angry."

34

Then, from the open window, the prince heard people shouting.

"What is it?" he asked. "What are they saying?"

Tom's father stuck his head out of the window, and laughed. "Well, well, well!" he said. "It seems our king is dead."

35

Silent tears slipped down Edward's face. "My father is dead," he whispered. "I am king now!"

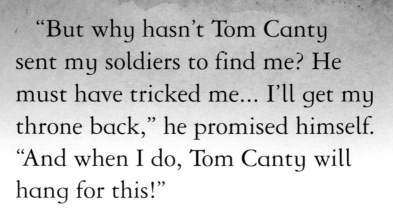

"But why hasn't Tom Canty sent my soldiers to find me? He must have tricked me... I'll get my throne back," he promised himself. "And when I do, Tom Canty will hang for this!"

That night, as the prince slept, Tom's mother crept over to him. "Can it really be true, what he said?" she wondered.

She lifted a candle and carried it over. Ever since Tom was little, he had always raised his hands to his face whenever he was shocked or startled from his dreams.

Breathing hard, Tom's mother
flashed the candle in front of the
sleeping prince. The sleeper's eyes
sprung open, but his hands hung
by his sides.

Tom's mother started back. "This
isn't my son!" she thought. "But he
must be." And with that, she too lay
down and fell into an uneasy sleep.

Chapter 4

Tom is king

"The king is dead?" whispered Tom, when he was told by Lord Hertford the next morning.

A stream of lords and ladies then entered the room. They stretched out their hands and cried, "Long live the king!"

"I am king now?" Tom gasped. "Does that mean any command I give will be obeyed?"

"Of course, Your Majesty," said Lord Hertford.

"Then hurry to the Tower," said Tom. "Tell them the king says the Duke of Norfolk shall not die."

A man rushed to obey his orders.

"A good start to a new reign," said Lord Hertford, smiling at him.

And everyone cried again, "Long live the king!"

After that, servants flooded into Tom's room. "Your Majesty," said a servant, bowing low, "it is time for you to dress."

Tom watched in amazement, as one servant, then another, knelt before him.

They slipped garment after garment over his head. It took an hour before he was fully dressed — in purple satin from top to toe.

43

"The date for your coronation
has been set," said Lord Hertford.
"It will take place three weeks from
now. There is just one small matter."

"W-w-what's that?" asked Tom.

"We have been unable to find
your father's Great Seal. Can you
tell us where it might be?"

"The Great Seal?" said Tom.
"What does it look like?"

Lord Hertford started and muttered to himself, "He doesn't know the Great Seal! He must still be out of his mind."

But aloud, he only said, "No matter, Your Majesty. I will leave you now. But I will see you tonight, of course, at the royal banquet."

All day, Tom had dreaded the banquet. "All the nobles will be there," he thought. "What will I say to them all? I'll be found out, for sure..."

But when he saw the glorious piles of food, he forgot his fear and fell on the food with his fingers.

No one said a word. They had all been warned not to comment on the king's table manners.

Tom stopped eating only to inspect his napkin – he had never seen such beautiful material.

"Please, take it away," he said to a servant. "I should hate to spill food on it."

At the end of the meal, a lord approached Tom with a golden bowl, filled with rosewater, for him to clean his fingers.

Tom looked confused for a
moment, then raised the bowl to
his lips and drank it all.

Still, no one said a word. After
that, Tom filled his pockets with
nuts and, exhausted, went straight
to bed.

Chapter 5

Coronation day

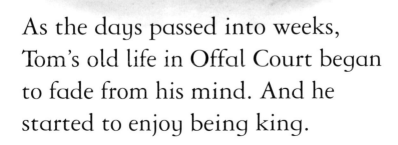

As the days passed into weeks,
Tom's old life in Offal Court began
to fade from his mind. And he
started to enjoy being king.

49

He watched the lords and ladies, and copied them...

...and he grew to love being waited on hand and foot...

...until one hundred servants didn't seem like enough to him, so he doubled them.

Tom woke on his coronation day with a smile on his lips. He could hear cheers from the crowd outside.

"The people of England have come to welcome me as king," he thought with pride.

Dressed in his coronation robes, Tom rode through the smiling crowd as if in a dream. "God save the king!" they shouted to him.

"God save you all!" Tom replied.

51

Edward stood within the sea of people. He watched Tom's approach with disbelief. "I will not let this happen!" he vowed.

With a sudden wriggle, he slipped from Tom's father's grasp, and disappeared into the heaving crowd. "Come back!" roared John Canty, stumbling after him.

Tom turned at the sound of his father's voice, and saw a white, astonished face. "My mother!" he realized. And, as always when startled, he raised his hands to shield his face.

In an instant, his mother tore through the crowd. "Oh my child! My darling!" she cried.

Tom heard himself say, "I don't know you. Don't come near me."

One of the king's soldiers snatched Tom's mother and pulled her away.

Tom watched her go. He saw the look she gave him – wounded, broken-hearted. "What have I done?" he thought.

More than anything, Tom longed to rush after his mother. "I'm not a king," he thought. "I'm a liar." But the procession went on – and Tom felt powerless to stop it.

He sat pale and still through the crowning ceremony. As the last act, the Archbishop lifted the crown of England from its cushion and held it over the trembling Tom.

"I forbid you to set the crown of England on that head. I am the king!" declared a barefoot, ragged boy.

Guards rushed to seize him. "No! Don't touch him!" cried Tom, throwing off his fur-lined cloak. "He is the king."

"It's his madness," said Lord Hertford. "Seize the urchin."

"No!" cried Tom again, stamping his foot. "I swear he is the king."

The guards didn't know which boy to turn to. Lord Hertford stepped forward, staring from Tom's face to Edward's, and back again. "Amazing!" he said.

"Which is the true king?" demanded the crowd.

"The Great Seal!" said Lord Hertford, looking at Edward. "Can you tell me where it is?"

"The Great Seal?" said Edward. "I don't know. Oh! I left it somewhere, but I don't know where..." As he spoke, he could feel the crowd turn against him.

"You *must* remember," urged Tom.
"What is it?"

"A great gold disk," said Edward.

"What? That thing! Now I know
where it is. You have to remember,
or they won't believe us. Think,
Your Majesty..."

"Yes!" cried Edward. "It's in my private cabinet. Go to the palace," he ordered a courtier. "You'll find it in the top jewel closet."

The courtier hesitated.

"What are you waiting for?" said Tom. "Go at once."

For half an hour, the crowd had to wait. The air was filled with frantic conversation, buzzing back and forth.

At last, the courtier returned.
There was a sudden hush. The
courtier raised his hand. In it, he
held the Great Seal. A shout went
up. "Long live the true king!"

"Now strip this pretender," ordered Lord Hertford. "And take him to the Tower to be hanged."

"No!" said Edward. "No one must touch him – for today he has acted like a king. And from now on, he and his family will live at the palace – except for his brute of a father."

The proud and happy Tom Canty knelt and kissed the king.

Then Edward spoke to the crowds. "I never knew what it was like to be poor," he said. "These past few weeks, I have been hungry, beaten, alone and afraid. From this day, I promise to be a friend to the poor."

"For now I know it to be true," he added to Tom in a whisper. "But for the accident of our birth, you could be me, and I could be you."

Mark Twain was a famous American writer, who lived over a hundred years ago. He wrote *The Prince and the Pauper* in 1882, although the story is set even further back in the past, in 1547. Twain based the prince in the story on Edward VI, who was a child king. Edward was nine years old when his father, King Henry VIII died, and he became King of England and Ireland. However, he only reigned for five and a half years. He died aged fifteen, of a lung disease.

Edward VI   *Mark Twain*

Series editor: Lesley Sims

Designed by Maria Pearson and Michelle Lawrence

First published in 2008 by Usborne Publishing Ltd., Usborne House, 83-85 Saffron Hill, London EC1N 8RT, England. www.usborne.com Copyright © 2008 Usborne Publishing Ltd.
Printed in China. UE. First published in America in 2008.